Contents

Introduction 5

1   Hand Washing 6

2   Vaccines 12

3   Antibiotics 18

4   Anaesthetics 25

5   X-Rays 32

6   Artificial Limbs 38

Epilogue 44

Timeline 46

Glossary 48

Selected Bibliography 49

Further Reading and Websites 50

Index 53

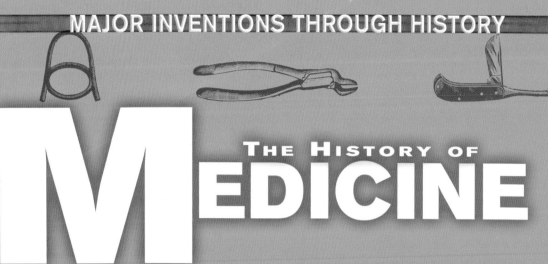

THE HISTORY OF
MEDICINE

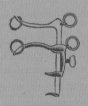

Michael Woods and Mary B Woods

Lerner Books
London • New York • Minneapolis

To the Rockefeller Foundation's Bellagio Study Centre in Italy, which helped launch our careers as authors of books for young readers

First published in the United Kingdom in 2009 by
Lerner Books,
Dalton House,
60 Windsor Avenue,
London SW19 2RR

Website address: www.lernerbooks.co.uk

This edition was updated and edited for UK publication by Discovery Books Ltd.,
Unit 3, 37 Watling Street, Leintwardine, Shropshire SY7 0LW

British Library Cataloguing in Publication Data

Woods, Michael, 1946-
The history of medicine. - 2nd ed. - (Major inventions
through history)
1. Medicine - History - Juvenile literature 2. Medical
innovations - History - Juvenile literature
I. Title II. Woods, Mary B.
610.9

ISBN-13: 978 1 58013 514 6

Printed in China

Introduction

For people born in the years before 1900, life was often short. Many people died before their fortieth birthday. Doctors weren't sure what caused diseases and there were few medicines to prevent or cure illness. Doctors performed operations with simple knives and few painkillers. Illnesses that modern medicines can cure easily often killed people.

In modern times, people in some countries can expect to live almost eighty years. People get fewer diseases than they did in earlier centuries. When people do get ill or hurt, they have to endure less pain and they recover sooner. Scientists have discovered substances that can prevent some diseases, and they have developed medicines that can treat and cure others.

In this book, we will learn about six super inventions that have helped people live longer, healthier, happier lives. You'll read about miracle drugs made from mould and learn how germs from a cow changed the world. You are about to begin an adventure in the history of medical inventions.

CHAPTER 1

Hand Washing

In 1840 a doctor cleaned an infected cut on a boy's arm. The doctor's hands were filthy with pus and blood from the wound. He wiped his hands on a dirty towel. Then he sewed up a girl's cut leg. Soon the girl's leg was also infected. What had happened?

Anton van Leeuwenhoek uses a
new invention, the microscope,
and sees germs.

1674

Germs from the boy's arm spread to the doctor's unwashed hands and then to the girl's leg. Germs are micro-organisms (tiny living things) that cause diseases. Germs include bacteria and viruses. The doctor in 1840 didn't know about bacteria and viruses. He didn't know he could kill these germs simply by washing his hands.

It's hard to imagine hand washing as an invention, but the doctor's realization that hand washing could prevent sickness was actually one of the greatest medical discoveries in history. How great was it?

GERMS EVERYWHERE

Before the 1900s, most people were used to being dirty. Few people had sinks or showers. To take a bath, people hauled buckets of water from a river or well and then heated the water over a fire. They used bowls and holes in the ground as toilets. Sometimes people dumped human waste outside. When it rained, the waste ran into rivers and lakes. The human waste was full of germs. Many people became ill when they drank germ-filled water.

Disease-causing staphylococcus bacteria (staph). As late as the 1800s, many doctors and scientists were unaware of the relationship between bacteria and illness.

Van Leeuwenhoek's discovery goes mostly unnoticed by the scientific and medical communities.
1600s–1800s

Some scientists use microscopes to begin to explore the world of micro-organisms.
1800s

In 2003 the US Centers for Disease Control and Prevention (CDC), a government agency, said that 'hand washing is the single most important means of preventing the spread of infection.'

Mystery on the Maternity Ward

In Vienna, Austria, a mysterious illness haunted hospitals in the 1840s. Women having babies entered the hospital healthy, but within a few days of giving birth, about 30 per cent of the new mothers had died from a disease called puerperal fever. In 1844 Ignaz Semmelweis, a doctor at one of the hospitals, discovered the cause. He noticed that women treated by doctors who washed their hands stayed healthy. Other women often got puerperal fever. Semmelweis realized that doctors were spreading the disease on their unwashed hands. In 1847 he ordered doctors at the hospital to wash their hands before touching patients. Deaths from puerperal fever fell to less than 11 percent.

Despite Dr Semmelweis's discovery, doctors at other hospitals did not want to wash their hands.

FAST FACT

Anton van Leeuwenhoek, a Dutch scientist, was the first person to identify germs. In the 1670s, he improved on the microscope, a new invention at the time. Microscopes are machines that make tiny objects look bigger. Leeuwenhoek's microscope could enlarge images up to 270 times their original size. He used his microscope to look at bacteria and other tiny life-forms.

Ignaz Semmelweis discovers that hand washing prevents the spread of infection.

1844

Semmelweis's hand washing policy for medical staff dramatically reduces death from infections.

1847

They thought that damp air caused diseases. They didn't know about germs, and they could not imagine how dirty hands could make people ill. Many doctors laughed at Dr Semmelweis's idea.

Putting Ideas into Action

Starting in the 1860s, scientists began to learn more about germs. Louis Pasteur, a French scientist,

HYGIENE: A NOVEL IDEA

Cleanliness improved in the 1900s. In Britain and many other nations, people began to install toilets, showers and sinks in their homes. Cities built sewage systems to carry away human waste. They built networks of pipes to bring pure drinking water to every home. Public health facilities improved and people learned more about how to keep clean and avoid germs. In modern times, we can buy dozens of different kinds of soap and other products that help us to keep clean.

Louis Pasteur in his lab.

Louis Pasteur studies bacteria and their relationship to infection, forming the 'germ theory' of disease.

1860s

DID YOU KNOW?

Germs get on people's hands in different ways. Always wash your hands: after using the toilet; after blowing your nose, sneezing or coughing; before eating or touching food; after touching uncooked meat; after changing a baby's nappy; after playing with pets; before touching your mouth, eyes or nose.

studied bacteria. He learned that some bacteria cause diseases. Around the same time, Joseph Lister, a Scottish doctor, invented an antiseptic, a liquid that kills bacteria. A few years later, Robert Koch, a German scientist, proved that specific bacteria cause specific diseases.

Doctors weren't laughing anymore. Convinced by the work of Pasteur, Koch and Lister, they began to use antiseptic on their hands and surgical instruments and made sure to wash their hands. Because of this, fewer patients got infections after surgery. Doctors still didn't wear sterile masks, gowns and gloves though.

Joseph Lister

Joseph Lister invents antiseptic. The liquid kills bacteria on contact.

1860s

Building on Pasteur's germ theory of disease, Robert Koch further proves that specific bacteria cause specific diseases.

1882

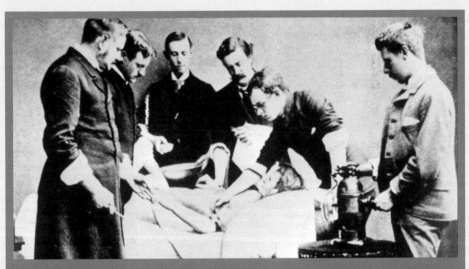

Surgeons and students perform surgery using antiseptic in the late 1800s. The man at the far right operates a mister, which sprays a fine mist of antiseptic on the patient and throughout the surgical area.

Modern-day operating rooms are super clean. Doctors scrub their hands for many minutes before operating on patients. They use special machines to sterilize their surgical tools and equipment. They wear sterile clothing, masks and rubber gloves. Dentists and other health-care professionals also wash their hands and use clean equipment and clothing when treating patients.

Pasteur and Koch prove germ theory. Doctors use antiseptic to sterilize their hands and surgical areas.

Doctors and other health-care givers scrub their hands and use sterilized equipment and clothing when treating patients.

late 1800s   **1900s–present**

CHAPTER 2

Vaccines

Hundreds of years ago, many people caught a disease called small-pox. Smallpox was caused by a virus, a type of germ. People who got the disease developed big, pus-filled sores all over their bodies and many of them died. Those lucky enough to survive the disease were left with deep scars, or pockmarks, on their faces.

In Europe, people noticed that milkmaids never got smallpox. Milkmaids were women who milked cows for a living. Their faces were always smooth and clear, without any pockmarks. Scientists

The first smallpox epidemic
is recorded in Egypt.

1350 BC

thought that milkmaids escaped smallpox because they caught a milder form of the disease from cows, called cowpox, which made people only slightly ill. Scientists thought that having cowpox gave people immunity to (protection from) smallpox.

In 1796 a British physician named Edward Jenner decided to test this theory. He infected a boy, James Phipps, with pus from the hand of a milkmaid who had cowpox.

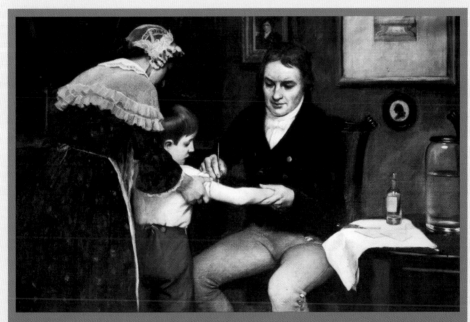

In this painting, Dr Edward Jenner *(sitting, right)* infects James Phipps *(centre)* with cowpox pus on 14 May 1796. Jenner hoped the vaccination would prevent Phipps from catching the more deadly smallpox.

Smallpox spreads to Europe, causing massive epidemics of the disease.

AD 600s

Edward Jenner tests his smallpox vaccine on James Phipps.

1796

James then developed cowpox. A month and a half later, Jenner infected James with pus from someone who had smallpox. James didn't get smallpox. The cowpox injection had prepared his body to fight off smallpox in the future. Jenner had created the first vaccine — an injection of dead or living germs that increases immunity to more dangerous germs.

This cartoon from 1802 shows Dr Jenner *(standing, left centre)* vaccinating people with cowpox. With cows growing from the characters, the cartoon shows people's fear of vaccinations.

Jenner's smallpox vaccine is successful, but many people fear awful side effects.

late 1790s

A US government poster from the 1940s urges parents to have their children vaccinated against smallpox.

IS YOUR CHILD VACCINATED?

Vaccination PREVENTS SMALLPOX

CHICAGO DEPARTMENT OF HEALTH

An Injection in the Arm

Gradually, other doctors began to use Jenner's invention. In the 1850s, countries in Europe passed laws requiring everyone to be vaccinated against smallpox. The United States passed a similar law in the early 1900s. The smallpox vaccine was administered in an injection, using a needle.

Scientists developed vaccines for other diseases, including cholera, tuberculosis (TB) and rabies. Governments in some countries passed laws requiring everyone to get vaccinations for these and other diseases. Vaccinations saved many lives and helped to keep people healthy.

Countries in Europe require all citizens to be vaccinated against smallpox.

1850s

Pasteur successfully uses his vaccine for rabies. Other vaccinations also are being developed at this time.

1885

Dr Jonas Salk

A Landmark Vaccine

Polio was a dreaded disease in earlier eras. Caused by a virus, the disease often damages its victims' legs. Some victims become paralysed, or unable to move parts of their bodies. Polio often strikes children. In the mid-1900s, people were especially fearful of polio in summer, when many children went swimming, because the polio virus can spread through unclean water. The thirty-second president of the US, Franklin D Roosevelt, who held office in the 1930s and 1940s, had polio. He couldn't walk without the help of a cane or leg braces.

Jonas Salk, a US scientist, invented the first polio vaccine in 1954. Albert Sabin, another American, invented a second, more effective vaccine in 1957. The polio vaccine wiped out polio in most countries.

FAST FACT

Death caused by polio is becoming increasingly rare. The World Health Organization (WHO) is working with governments to vaccinate everybody against the disease.

Jonas Salk develops the
first vaccine for polio.

1954

Vaccination Worldwide

Although vaccines eliminated many diseases in Britain and other well-off nations, people in many developing countries could not afford vaccines for smallpox and other diseases. In the 1900s, smallpox killed up to 500 million people around the world.

In the 1970s, the United Nations started giving free smallpox vaccinations in poor countries. The programme was a success. It had entirely wiped out smallpox by 1980. In the early 2000s, the smallpox virus exists only in scientific laboratories.

In modern times, scientists have vaccines for many diseases. Doctors vaccinate babies for mumps, measles and other illnesses. Many children and adults get yearly vaccines for influenza (the flu). Scientists hope to develop more vaccines in the future.

FUTURE VACCINES: BITE ME

Getting vaccinated usually involves a little ouch! Most vaccines are injected with a sharp needle – and that hurts. However, scientists are working on creating vaccines that you can eat. Scientists want to grow special genetically engineered plants (plants with altered genes) that contain vaccines. With this invention, people could get vaccines in a bite of banana or a forkful of rice. This kind of vaccine could improve vaccination programmes in developing countries. Vaccine-containing plants could be grown right where they are needed. Scientists think edible vaccines might also work better than injected vaccines.

An extensive global vaccination programme wipes out smallpox in the human population.

1980

CHAPTER 3

Antibiotics

Have you ever taken a miracle drug? If you've ever had an antibiotic, the answer is yes. Many children take antibiotics for ear infections and sore throats. If you've ever had a dangerous infection, an antibiotic may have saved your life.

Antibiotics are chemicals that stop bacteria from growing inside the body. By stopping the growth of bacteria, antibiotics can stop infections and cure diseases. In modern times, antibiotics are common, inexpensive medicines. People usually take them in tablet form. Though they might look simple, antibiotics are wonder drugs. They are also one of the most important inventions in medical history.

Searching for Magic Bullets

People have always used medicines to treat illness and injury. Thousands of years ago in ancient Egypt, people smeared a paste of honey and animal fat on cuts and wounds. Native Americans applied mould and other kinds of fungus to their wounds. Some of these treatments worked, but

> ### WHAT'S IN A NAME
> The term *antibiotic* comes from two Greek words: *anti*, which means 'against,' and *bio*, which means 'life.' The name refers to antibiotics' ability to kill living bacteria.

people didn't know why. Some people thought the treatments were magic, driving away evil spirits that caused illness.

In the late 1800s, scientists learned that germs caused many diseases. Scientists started searching for medicines to kill those germs. In 1928 Alexander Fleming, a Scottish scientist, was growing some staphylococcus bacteria in his laboratory. This kind of bacteria causes serious infections.

Fleming noticed something odd on a plate where some staph was growing. A mould had also started to grow on the plate. Much

Alexander Fleming discovers a
mould that can kill bacteria –
the first antibiotic.

1928

FAST FACT

Antibiotics can kill only bacteria, one kind of germ. They are not effective against viruses, another kind of germ.

to Fleming's surprise, the staph around the mould had died. Fleming realized that the mould, *Penicillium notatum*, released a liquid that killed bacteria. He had discovered the first antibiotic. Fleming named the new drug penicillin. Doctors used it to treat scarlet fever, pneumonia and other diseases caused by bacteria.

The penicillin mould grew slowly though, and it took a large amount of mould to make a small amount of medicine. By 1939 the need for penicillin was urgent. World War II (1939–1945) had

Dr Alexander Fleming observes the effects of *Penicillium notatum* (penicillin) on bacteria in a petri dish in the late 1920s.

started in Europe and thousands of soldiers were dying from infected wounds. In 1941 scientists invented a way to make big batches of penicillin.

The new drug saved many lives, especially on World War II battlefields. Penicillin truly was a wonder drug. Doctors called it a magic bullet, because it cured serious illnesses without causing major side effects, unless a person was allergic to it.

Miracle Drugs versus Super Bugs

In the second half of the 1900s, scientists discovered many more antibiotics. Doctors needed different kinds of antibiotics because antibiotics don't all work the same. Penicillin, for instance, works on some infections but not others. Doctors needed different antibiotics for different diseases. In addition, antibiotics can slowly lose their effectiveness against germs. Over time, germs can change their genetic form (basic

MEDICINE FROM DIRT

With the discovery of penicillin, scientists started to look for other moulds that could produce antibiotics. Many moulds live in the soil, so scientists collected and checked soil samples. They succeeded in finding serveral other moulds that produced antibiotics.

One of these moulds, streptomyces, saves millions of lives each year. It was the first treatment for tuberculosis, a serious lung disease. Selman Waksman, a US scientist, discovered the antibiotic streptomycin in 1943. Scientists still search the dirt for new antibiotics. They also make new antibiotics from chemicals in the laboratory.

Scientists learn to make large amounts of penicillin, saving the lives of many soldiers fighting in World War II.

1941

Selman Waksman discovers streptomycin, a treatment for tuberculosis.

1943

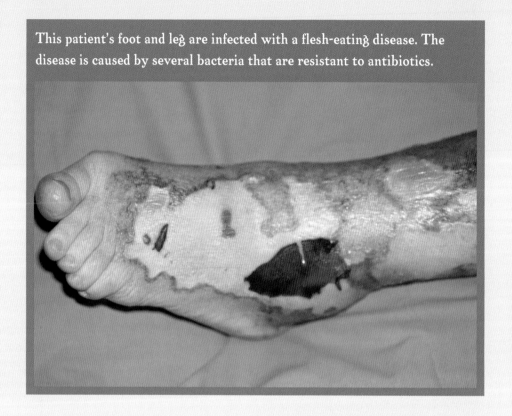

This patient's foot and leg are infected with a flesh-eating disease. The disease is caused by several bacteria that are resistant to antibiotics.

FAST FACT

When treating patients, modern doctors have many different antibiotics to choose from. New antibiotics are constantly being developed.

chemical make-up), developing resistance to antibiotics that once killed them. Called super bugs, these new forms of germs shrug off (resist) big doses of antibiotics that once would have worked quickly. As germs

Scientists report the first form of staph infection that is resistant to penicillin.

1945

As this American poster from the 1930s shows, diseases such as pneumonia were very deadly before antibiotics.

change, scientists must keep developing many new kinds of antibiotics to fight them.

Lifesaving Medicines

How did antibiotics change the world? Antibiotics save lives. Before antibiotics, pneumonia, a disease which affects the lungs, was a major cause of death. However, since the invention of antibiotics, most patients who get pneumonia will recover.

Antibiotics also save money. Millions of people get infections each year. Before antibiotics, many people had to spend weeks in the hospital recovering from infections. Hospital stays and treatments were often very expensive.

A BELLYFUL OF GERMS

Stomach ulcers are sores inside the stomach. They bleed and ache. Doctors once thought that stress and spicy foods caused ulcers. There was no cure. Some patients with ulcers stayed in the hospital for long periods. They had to swallow nasty tasting medicine and sometimes doctors had to operate to remove patients' ulcers. In 1986 scientists found out that bacteria cause stomach ulcers. After this discovery, doctors began treating some people with ulcers with antibiotics instead of surgery and other medicines.

With the invention of antibiotics, most people can recover at home, taking antibiotics in tablet form.

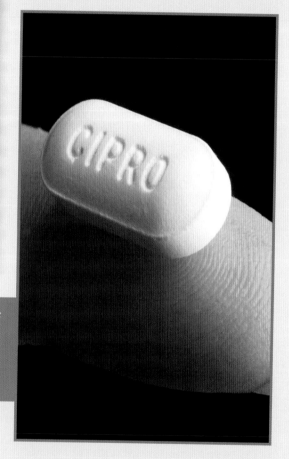

One of the latest generations of antibiotics, Cipro (ciprofloxacin hydrochloride), has worked well on antibiotic-resistant bacteria.

Scientists discover that bacteria cause stomach ulcers, which means ulcers can be treated with antibiotics.

1986

CHAPTER 4

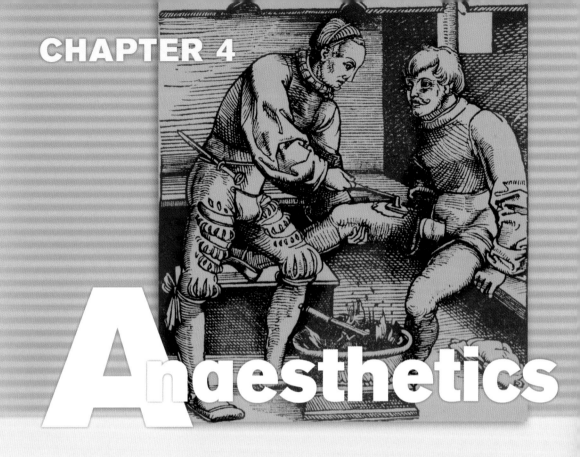

Anaesthetics

In 1841 a man needed an operation for cancer of the tongue. With one stroke of a knife, Dr John Collins Warren cut off the tip of the man's tongue. Dr Warren then touched a red-hot iron to the cut to stop the bleeding.

Wide awake, the patient felt it all. Wild with pain, he jumped up and ran away from the operating table. Dr Warren's assistants caught him. Again, the doctor administered the hot iron to stop the bleeding. As the man squirmed, the iron burned his lips, making the pain worse.

The man felt the whole operation because at that time doctors had no anaesthetics — medicines to numb pain. So it is no wonder patients dreaded having surgery.

Early Anaesthetics

Before the mid-1800s, doctors had few effective treatments for pain. To ease the pain of surgery, some doctors punched patients in the jaw to knock them unconscious. Other doctors got their patients drunk with whisky or gave them dangerous drugs such as opium.

DR FAST, DR FASTER AND DR FASTEST

Before anaesthetics, the best surgeon was a fast surgeon. Since patients felt horrible pain during surgery, operations had to be done fast. Some surgeons boasted that they could cut off an arm in a minute. Even the best surgeons could not work fast enough to avoid inflicting pain. Patients would scream in agony. They had to be tied to the operating table or held down by strong men. Anaesthetics put an end to all that suffering.

Alcohol vapour anaesthesia, 1500s.

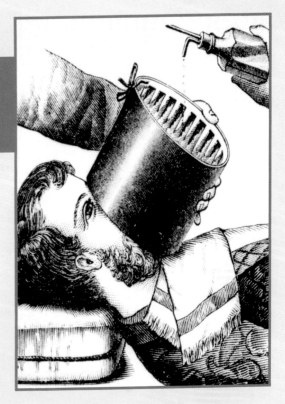

A patient inhales ether vapour prior to an operation in the 1800s.

These treatments were only slightly effective in numbing the pain of surgery.

In 1799 the British scientist Humphry Davy experimented with a gas called nitrous oxide. He found that inhaling the gas relieved pain. Davy called nitrous oxide 'laughing gas' because people got giggly after breathing it. In 1818 Michael Faraday, another British scientist, discovered that the vapour (fumes) of a liquid called ether had similar effects.

In 1842 Dr Crawford Long, a physician from Georgia, USA, had a patient inhale ether vapours before surgery. The ether made the patient unconscious and insensitive to the pain. Dr Long did not announce his discovery and so other doctors knew nothing about it.

Humphry Davy uses nitrous oxide ('laughing gas') to relieve pain during surgery.

1799

In 1844 Horace Wells, a dentist from Connecticut, USA, inhaled nitrous oxide himself before having a tooth pulled out. He fell unconscious and felt no pain during the procedure. Unlike Dr Long, Dr Wells told others about his experience.

The next doctor to use ether was William Morton, an American dentist. On 18 October 1846, Dr Morton had a surgical patient inhale ether vapour. Then surgeons operated on the man in front of a big audience of doctors and medical students. The man slept peacefully as the surgeon cut into his neck. It was amazing! The operation was totally painless.

The news spread fast and other doctors began using ether. It was not without problems, however, as patients often felt very sick and vomited after waking from ether anaesthesia. Nevertheless, ether allowed doctors to perform operations slowly, not worrying that their patients might feel pain.

The development of ether anaesthesia led scientists to invent even better anaesthetics. One of the most important was sodium pentothal. Two scientists, Ernest Volwiler and Donalee Tabern, from the USA, developed this drug in 1936. Sodium pentothal was

BRAIN TEASER

Can pain be good for you? Actually, *some* pain is good. Pain can be a natural warning signal that something is wrong. It can alert you to take action to avoid more danger. For instance, pain can warn you: 'That pot is hot! Take your finger away before you get burnt,' or 'Don't run on that sprained ankle. You'll hurt it even more.'

William Morton demonstrates the use of ether to a team of doctors and medical students.

1846

Dr Morton *(second from top on the right)* and other medical staff re-enact the successful use of ether anaesthesia for surgery in 1850. Others had successfully used ether prior to Morton's demonstration in October 1846.

the first anaesthetic that could be injected into the body in liquid form. It worked fast and patients fell asleep in seconds.

Homing in on Pain

Ether, nitrous oxide and sodium pentothal are called general anaesthetics. They put patients to sleep and block pain all over the body. Sometimes, however, doctors don't want to make patients unconscious during treatments. For instance, women having babies often want, and need, to stay awake during the birth. In this case doctors give women anaesthetics that allow them to stay awake, but block

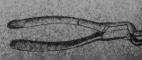

ANCIENT WISDOM

In ancient times, doctors in Egypt, Greece, Rome and other lands knew how to make painkilling drugs from plants. Some ancient Chinese doctors used a procedure called acupuncture to treat pain. They stuck thin needles into certain areas of the body, relieving pain in other parts of the body. Some modern doctors also use acupuncture to treat pain and other health problems.

pain in the lower part of the body. Medicines that block pain in one area are called local anaesthetics.

Local anaesthetics are less powerful than general anaesthetics. They take less time to wear off, allowing patients to return to their regular lives sooner. One of the most commonly used local anaesthetics is novocaine, invented by a German scientist, Alfred Einhorn, in 1905.

No More Ouch!

How has anaesthesia changed people's lives? Think about having to get a tooth filled — or pulled — before anaesthetics were discovered. It would hurt. There were no medicines to take away the pain of drilling or pulling teeth. Many people were afraid to go to the dentist. Their teeth often rotted and ached, but they

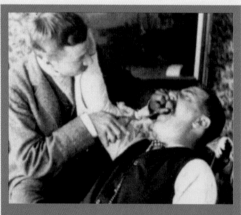

Dentistry without novocaine, 1890.

Alfred Einhorn invents
novocaine, a common
local anaesthetic.

1905

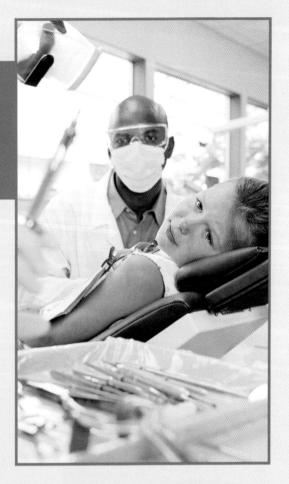

A girl about to receive novocaine from a dentist. Though she may feel some pain from the needle, the drug will keep her pain free during the dental procedure.

still didn't get treatment. By the age of thirty, some people had lost all their teeth.

Then think about going to the dentist for a filling in modern times. The dentist first puts a liquid anaesthetic on your gums (the pink tissue surrounding your teeth). This anaesthetic keeps you from fully feeling the pain from an injection of local anaesthetic. This injection numbs your tooth, so the dentist can drill out the tooth decay painlessly.

American scientists develop sodium pentothal, the first anaesthetic that can be injected in liquid form.

1936

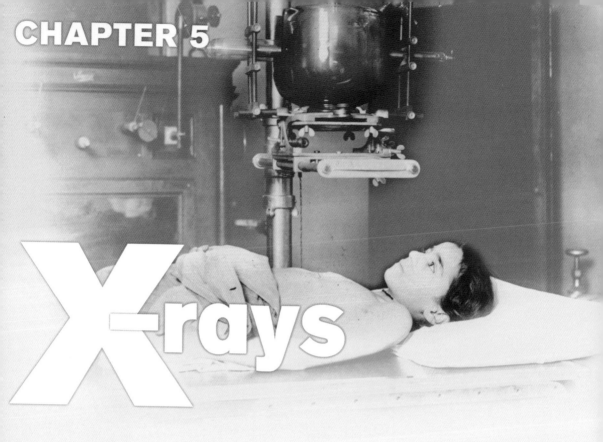

CHAPTER 5

X-rays

Suppose you banged into another player during a football match. Doctors might want to see if you had a broken leg. To do this they would use one of the most amazing medical inventions: the X-ray.

Few other medical inventions can do so much. X-rays can diagnose broken bones, cancer and many other health problems. Doctors also use X-rays as a treatment. For instance, X-rays can slow or stop the growth of cancer cells.

X-rays can't be seen with the human eye. Nobody can feel them with a fingertip. X-rays are pure energy. They are like light, radio waves and the microwaves that pop popcorn.

Is That Screen *Glowing*?

A German scientist named Wilhelm Roentgen discovered X-rays by accident in 1895. He was studying radiation, a kind of energy, given off by a cathode-ray tube (similar to an old TV picture tube).

Roentgen turned the tube on. Then he glanced at a glass screen a metre or so away. The screen was glowing. He turned the tube off. The glow disappeared. He turned it back on. The glow reappeared. The tube was giving off invisible rays! They passed through the air and made the screen's surface glow. Roentgen didn't know what they were. He named them X-rays.

William Roentgen

The Bones in Bertha's Hand

Next, Roentgen's hand accidentally got in the way of the X-ray beam. He was shocked when he saw the screen. Glowing there was an image of the bones inside his

hand. Roentgen had discovered that X-rays pass through human flesh, but not bone. That's why the bones left an image, like a shadow, on the screen.

Roentgen asked his wife, Bertha, to put her hand on photographic film. Then he exposed her hand to X-rays. When the film was developed, it showed an image of the bones in Bertha's hand. That photograph was the first X-ray picture. News about X-rays spread quickly. Doctors around the world began using X-rays to see inside the body.

A Window on the Body

X-rays allow doctors to see inside the body — literally. An X-ray of a

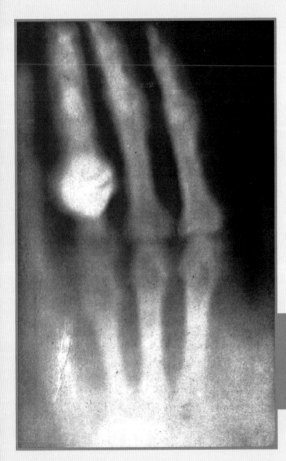

Roentgen's first X-ray of his wife Bertha's hand. Bertha's hand bones and wedding ring are visible.

Wilhelm Roentgen makes an X-ray of his wife's hand. The picture shows her bones and wedding ring.

1895

Wilhelm Roentgen receives the first Nobel Prize in Physics.

1901

broken bone helps doctors to work out the best way to set it. X-rays of the chest tell doctors whether people have serious lung diseases such as tuberculosis or lung cancer. X-rays help doctors identify cancer and other life-threatening diseases early — often before a person has any symptoms, or outward signs of disease. By catching diseases early, X-rays help doctors save thousands of lives each year.

X-rays also make surgery much simpler. Before X-rays, surgeons often had to guess where to make their incisions. For example, if they needed to remove a bullet, they simply cut and cut until they found it. With X-rays, surgeons can see the exact location of diseased tissue, bones and foreign objects, such as bullets. X-rays enable doctors to make their incisions at exactly the right place.

X-rays help dentists too. By X-raying patients' teeth, dentists can find tooth decay in areas that are hard to see with the eye. Dentists can also tell if the roots of a patient's teeth are healthy.

X-Ray Vision

After Wilhelm Roentgen discovered X-rays, people got excited by the mysterious new rays. Writers began putting X-rays into their comic books, television programmes, and films. For instance, Superman, the famous comic book character, was said to have X-ray vision. He could see right through walls. In some stories, X-rays turned people and animals into monsters. However, none of these stories about X-rays were scientifically accurate.

PET X-Rays

PET scanning, or positron emission tomography, is a kind of computerized X-ray process. Other X-rays show only how the body looks inside. PET scans show how chemicals are acting inside the brain and other organs. Different kinds of chemical activity show up as different colours on a PET scan. By studying PET scans, doctors can tell whether or not the brain or another organ is working properly.

Better X-Rays

The first X-rays weren't perfect. For example, they could not make clear pictures of soft, non-bony parts of the body, such as the heart, the stomach and other organs. Then scientists invented special dyes that show up on X-rays. Other scientists invented ways to inject the dyes into the body. These dyes made it possible for soft structures to show up clearly on X-rays.

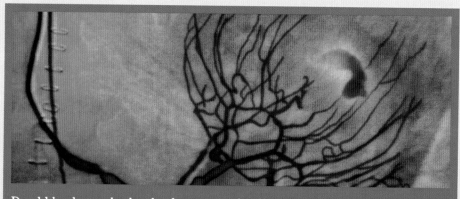

Dyed blood vessels clearly show up in this X-ray of a human stomach. Dyes help doctors X-ray soft tissues. Here, bleeding shows up as a red stain.

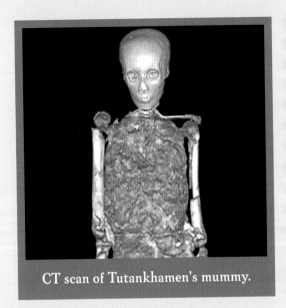

CT scan of Tutankhamen's mummy.

Oh, Mummy!

X-rays and CT scans are not just for doctors. They also let scientists see inside mummies from ancient Egypt and other lands. Mummies are dead bodies that have been preserved with fluids and then wrapped in layers of cloth. Scientists who study mummies don't want to cut into them and destroy them. Instead, they use X-rays and CT scans to make pictures of the mummies' bones and bodies without doing any damage. These have revealed health problems, such as tooth decay and broken bones.

CT scanning was another important invention. CT stands for computed tomography. Regular X-rays look flat, like the pictures in a book. CT scanners turn regular X-rays into lifelike, three-dimensional pictures. Allan Cormack of the United States and Godfrey Hounsfield from Britain invented CT scanning in 1972.

Although they save lives, X-rays can also be dangerous. Exposure to too many X-rays can cause cancer and other health problems. When they are needed to help an ill person, however, X-rays are often worth the risk. Doctors use X-rays only when they are needed.

Allan Cormack and Godfrey Hounsfield invent CT scanning.

1972

CHAPTER 6

Artificial Limbs

Captain Hook, the pirate in *Peter Pan* (a play and novel), had a steel hook instead of a hand. Long John Silver, a pirate in the book *Treasure Island*, walked on a wooden leg. Artificial (human-made) limbs like those described in these books were really used in the past. They were simply made. They did not work very well. Nevertheless, they enabled people without their own limbs to lead a normal life. Millions of people have artificial limbs. Some were born without arms or legs or with limbs that didn't work properly.

Others lost limbs in accidents or wars. Still others had diseases that could be treated only by amputation (cutting off an arm or leg). Losing a limb makes it hard to do the simplest things: just try dressing yourself with one hand. However, people who have lost limbs can live quite well, thanks to prosthetic (artificial) limbs.

Modern prosthetic limbs can do more than just snare things, like Captain Hook's hook hand. They can do more than just support a person's weight, like Long John Silver's wooden leg. Modern artificial limbs work like natural limbs. The fingers on an artificial hand, for example, can pick up objects. The knees and ankles on artificial legs can flex and turn just like real body parts. Modern artificial limbs are lightweight, strong, and comfortable to use. They look natural, much like real arms and legs.

> ### FAST FACT
> The technical name for an artificial limb is a prosthesis, or a prosthetic limb.

He Cut Off His Foot

Nobody knows when the first artificial limb was made. An ancient Greek historian, Herodotus, wrote about one early artificial limb in about 500 BC. Herodotus told about a prisoner who escaped from chains by cutting off his own foot. He later walked with a wooden foot. In 1858 archaeologists dug up the oldest artificial limb ever found. It was a leg made of copper and wood, made in about 300 BC.

Archaeologists find an artificial leg dating to about 300 BC

1858

This illustration from the 1700s shows wooden arms and wooden legs. Early artificial limbs were heavy and often difficult to use.

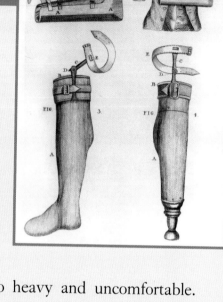

Some early artificial legs were made of a leather cup attached to a wooden peg. The cup fitted over the stump — the remaining part of the wearer's leg. Straps attached the cup to the wearer's body. Artificial arms and hands were made the same way.

The first artificial limbs were stiff and did not have joints that bent like real arms and legs. They were also heavy and uncomfortable. People could wear them only for short periods. Moreover, the straps often came undone and the limbs fell off.

Better Artificial Limbs

Ambroise Pare, a French surgeon, invented movable artificial limbs around 1580. One was a hand operated by springs, which pulled the fingers tight around objects. Another was a leg with a movable knee joint. In 1863 Dubois Parmelee of New York City, USA, invented a way to attach artificial limbs to the body using suction, a sort of vacuum action. Limbs attached with suction stayed on better and were more comfortable than those attached by straps.

Wars created a need for even better artificial limbs. During the US Civil War (1861–1865) and World War I (1914–1918), thousands of wounded soldiers had to have arms or legs amputated. To help these soldiers, inventors began to build artificial limbs from stronger, lighter materials.

Phantom Limbs

For a while after an amputation, people may feel pain and other feelings in the part of the body that's no longer there. Doctors call this sensation phantom limb pain. It happens because the brain does not yet realize that part of the body is gone.

By the mid-1900s, designers were making artificial limbs from superstrong plastics and metals like those used in spacecraft. Designers used electronics and computers to make artificial limbs work even better.

High-Tech Arms and Legs

In the 1960s, inventors worked out how to make artificial limbs controlled by myoelectricity — the electricity produced inside human muscles. These artificial limbs have sensors that pick up

Dubois Parmelee devises
a way to attach artificial
limbs using suction.

1863

electrical signals from the wearer's body. For instance, a wearer might flex a shoulder muscle, sending electrical signals to a motor in an artificial hand. The motor then makes the hand's fingers pinch.

One of the most famous artificial limbs is the Utah Arm, created in 1981 at the University of Utah. The Utah Arm is made from electronic and mechanical parts. The arm's elbow, wrist and fingers all move like natural body parts. With this arm, the wearer can pick up a raw egg and hold it securely, but not so tightly that the eggshell cracks.

In 2003 doctors at the Rehabilitation Institute of Chicago, in the USA, made another great advance in artificial limbs. They developed a prosthetic arm that could be controlled by a patient's thoughts. This

Wearing a Utah Arm (*right arm*), a mother plays with her baby. The bionic limb looks and works almost like a natural limb.

Scientists at the University of Utah create the lifelike Utah Arm.
1981

arm takes advantage of the electrical connections that already exist in the human nervous system. When the wearer thinks about bending the arm, the brain sends an electrical signal through the nerves to electrical devices in the arm.

Living without Limbs

Thanks to artificial limbs, people who lose a limb can still have full, active lives. In 2006 Mark Inglis, a mountaineer from New Zealand, became the first double amputee (a person who has had two of their limbs amputated) to climb to the summit of Mount Everest, the world's highest mountain, at 8,850 metres.

CYBORGS

In the 1970s, *The Six Million Dollar Man* and *The Bionic Woman* TV shows featured humans with artificial body parts. Because of their mechanical body parts, these characters had superhuman powers. Newer films, TV programmes and computer games feature characters called cyborgs. They, too, are part human and part machine.

Doctors at the Rehabilitation Institute of Chicago create an artificial limb that can be controlled by the wearer's thoughts.

2003

Epilogue

Cathy cut her foot on a sharp piece of glass at the beach. It became infected. She needed crutches to help her walk. Did she need an antibiotic, a medicine to treat the infection? No! Not in 2025!

Instead, the doctor called in the robots — 100 billion zillion tiny robots. The doctor gave Cathy a shot in the arm. It put billions of 'nanomachines' into her blood.

Anything called 'nano' is very, very small. For example, one nanosecond is a billionth of a second. The robots the doctor used to treat Cathy in the fictional scenario above were so small that four-hundred of them would fit across a human hair. The nanomachines had microscopic gears, linkages and wheels, just like big machines.

When the tiny machines reached the infection, some of them attacked the bacteria that were making Cathy ill. Others repaired the damage caused by the bacteria. She could soon walk normally again.

Nanotechnology is just one of many new technologies that will help doctors prevent, diagnose and treat diseases in the future. Some nanomachines may be robot surgeons, who could work to clear away fatty deposits blocking an artery, for instance. Other nanomachines might have tiny sensors, almost like microscopic smoke detectors. The machines will attach to cells inside the body. When a disease starts, the sensors will send a signal. Doctors will be able to treat the disease before it spreads and gets worse. Some nanomachines will attach to and destroy cancer cells. Others will act like tablets that deliver medicine only to diseased parts of the body. Nanomachines will be injected into the body using a needle. They will repair diseased organs from the inside, without any pain or incisions. People in the future will benefit from amazing bionic body parts. Bionics is the use of electronic devices and machines to replace parts of the human body. Bionic artificial limbs will become more natural. People will even use their thoughts to make an artificial leg or arm move. People with disabilities will benefit from bionic eyes, ears and other body parts. These electronic devices will connect to nerves in the body and will work almost like natural organs.

Some day, scientists hope that bionic artificial limbs won't even be necessary. Instead, scientists want to grow new body parts to replace those damaged by accidents or disease. Genetic engineering may make this possible. Genes are substances that control how the body works and grows. Scientists already know how to engineer (change and design) genes to grow new skin and other body tissue. In the future, scientists may discover how to grow whole limbs.

Some future medical inventions sound far-fetched. Imagine transplanting a human head onto a different person's body. Or tablets that make people more intelligent, or hearts grown in a laboratory for transplants. Imagine giving people a gene that lets them eat without getting fat or live to age 125. Such ideas may sound like science fiction, but scientists are already working on them.

1674 Anton van Leeuwenhoek is the first person to see germs, or micro-organisms, through a microscope.

1796 Edward Jenner invents the first vaccine. It protects James Phipps from smallpox.

1799 Humphry Davy discovers that inhaling nitrous oxide ('laughing gas') relieves pain.

1818 Michael Faraday discovers that inhaled ether vapour relieves pain.

1844 Ignaz Semmelweis discovers that hand washing prevents the spread of disease. Horace Wells uses nitrous oxide to prevent pain during the pulling of teeth.

1846 William Morton gives ether to a patient to prevent pain during surgery.

1863 Dubois Parmelee experiments with attaching artificial limbs to the body by suction.

1865 Joseph Lister develops an antiseptic spray to kill germs.

1882 Robert Koch proves that the tuberculosis (TB) germ causes TB.

1885 Louis Pasteur successfully uses his rabies vaccine, saving the life of Joseph Meister.

1895 Wilhelm Roentgen discovers X-rays.

1905 Alfred Einhorn invents a local anaesthetic called novocaine.

1921 The first tuberculosis vaccine is invented.

1928 Alexander Fleming discovers penicillin.

1936 Ernest Volwiler and Donalee Tabern invent sodium pentothal.

1941 Scientists develop a way to make penicillin in large amounts.

1943 Selman Waksman discovers streptomycin, the first antibiotic for treating TB.

1954 Jonas Salk creates the first polio vaccine.

1957 Albert Sabin creates the second polio vaccine.

1963 The vaccine for common measles goes into use.

1972 Allan Cormack and Godfrey Hounsfield invent computed to-mography (CT scans).

1981 The Utah Arm, a myoelectric artificial arm, is invented at the University of Utah.

1986 The germs that cause stomach ulcers are discovered.

2003 Doctors at the Rehabilitation Institute of Chicago, in America, develop a bionic arm that can be controlled by a patient's thoughts.

2005 Advances in nanotechnology improve building materials, clothing, and consumer products. Research into nanotechnology continues, with the possible future development of nanobots.

2006 Mark Inglis climbs Mount Everest on two artificial legs.

GLOSSARY

amputees: people who have had a limb or limbs amputated

anaesthetics: substances that cause a loss of pain or other feeling. Some anaesthetics cause people to lose consciousness

antibiotics: chemicals that stop bacteria from growing inside the body

antiseptic: a liquid or other substance that kills germs

bacteria: micro-organisms found in living things, soil, water and other substances. Some bacteria cause disease

genetic engineering: altering the genes, or basic chemical make-up, of a living thing

germs: micro-organisms that cause disease

immunity: protection from, or resistance to, a certain disease

infected: filled with germs or disease

micro-organism: a tiny living thing, such as a bacteria. Some micro-organisms can cause disease

prosthesis: an artificial limb

vaccine: a preparation, often administered as an injection, that gives a person immunity, or resistance, to a certain disease

viruses: micro-organisms that live inside another living thing. Viruses often cause disease

Selected Bibliography

Adler, Robert E. *Medical Firsts: From Hippocrates to the Human Genome*. New York: John Wiley & Sons, 2004.

Darling, David. *Beyond 2000: The Health Revolution, Surgery and Medicine in the Twenty-First Century*. Parsippany, NJ: Dillon Press, 1996.

Harrison, Peter. *All about Inventions: Amazing Breakthroughs That Shaped Our World*. London: Anness Publishing, Ltd, 2000.

Ingpen, Robert R. *Encyclopedia of Ideas That Changed the World: The Greatest Discoveries and Inventions of Human History*. Surrey, UK: Dragon's World, 1993.

Jeffrey, Kirk. *Machines in Our Hearts: The Cardiac Pacemaker, the Implantable Defibrillator, and American Health Care*. Baltimore: Johns Hopkins University Press, 2001.

Leikin, Jerrold B. *American Medical Association Complete Medical Encyclopedia*. New York: Random House Reference, 2003.

McGrew, Roderick E. *Encyclopedia of Medical History*. New York: McGraw-Hill, 1985.

Null, Gary. *Germs, Biological Warfare, Vaccinations: What You Need to Know*. New York: Seven Stories Press, 2003.

Porter, Roy. *Blood and Guts: A Short History of Medicine*. New York: Norton, 2002.

FURTHER READING AND WEBSITES

Books

Ballard, Carol. *From Cowpox to Antibiotics: Discovering Vaccines and Medicines* (Chain Reactions) 2006.

Claybourne, Anna. *World's Worst Germs: Micro-organisms and Disease* (Raintree Fusion) Raintree, 2005.

De La Bedoyere, Guy. *The First Polio Vaccination* (Milestones in Modern Science) Evans Brothers, 2005.

Goldsmith, Connie. *Cutting Edge Medicine* (Cool Science) Lerner, 2008.

Grady, Dennis and Richard Walker. *Epidemics and Plagues* (Kingfisher Knowledge) Kingfisher Books Ltd, 2006.

Farndon, John. *From Laughing Gas to Face Transplants: Discovering Transplant Surgery* (Chain Reactions) Heinemann Library, 2006.

Fullick, Ann. *Frontiers of Surgery* (Science at the Edge), Heinemann Library, 2006.

Jango-Cohen, Judith. *Bionics* (Cool Science), Lerner, 2008.

Johnson, Rebecca L. *Nanotechnology* (Cool Science), Lerner, 2008.

Kerrod, Robin. *Medicine* (Twenty-First Century Science) Franklin Watts Ltd., 2004.

Lassieur, Allison. *Louis Pasteur: Revolutionary Scientist* (Great Life Stories: (Inventors and Scientists) Franklin Watts Ltd., 2005.

Parker, Steve. *Alexander Fleming* (Groundbreakers: Scientists and Inventors) Heinemann, 2003.

Rooney, Anne. *Medicine: Stem Cells, Genes and Superbeams* (Cutting Edge), Heinemann Library, 2006.

Routh, Kristina. *Medicine* (Technology All Around Us) Franklin Watts Ltd., 2005.

Snedden, Robert. *DNA and Genetic Engineering* (Cells and Life) Heinemann Library 2008.

Tames, Richard. *Penicillin* (Turning Points in History) Heinemann, 2007.

Townsend, John. *Pills, Powders and Potions: A History of Medication* (Freestyle Express), Raintree, 2006.

Townsend, John. *Pox, Pus and Plague: A History of Disease and Infection*, (Painful History of Medicine (Freestyle Express) Raintree, 2006.

Websites

The Science Museum

http://www.sciencemuseum.org.uk/onlinestuff/subjects/medicine_and_biology.aspx

This website is a great place to learn about the developments and defining
moments in medicine. You can explore medical technology and find out
how wars and conflicts have impacted on medicine.

BBC Bitesize

http://www.bbc.co.uk/schools/gcsebitesize/history/shp/

Use this site to revise your knowledge of medicine through the ages.
Bitesize includes information on Egyptian, Roman, Renaissance and
modern medicine.

Children First for health

http://www.childrenfirst.nhs.uk

This website is packed with information on a wide range of medical topics,
including history of medicine, A-Z of illnesses and a body tour.

INDEX

acupuncture 30

amputate, amputation, amputee(s) 39, 41, 43

anaesthesia 28, 29, 30.

anaesthetic(s) 25-30: general, 29; liquid, 28, 29, 31; local, 29-30. *See also* ether anaesthesia; novocaine; sodium pentothal

antibiotic(s) 18-24, 44, 46: mass production of, 24; resistance to, 21-22. *See also* mould; Penicillium notatum

antiseptic 10-11, 46

bacteria 7-8, 10, 18-20, 22, 24, 44

Bertha's hand 33-34

bionics 45: bionic limb, 42, 45, 47

bleeding and blood, 6, 25: blood vessels, 36

bones 33-34, 35, 37: broken, 32

brain 36

cancer 32, 37, 45: cancer, lung, 35

cathode-ray tube 33

chemicals 18, 21, 36

children 16-18

cholera 15

cleanliness 6-11

computed tomography (CT) 37, 47

computers 36, 41, 43

Cormack, Allan 37, 47

cure 5, 19, 21, 24

cyborgs 43

Davy, Humphry 27, 46

dentist(s) 11, 28, 30-31, 35

design and designers 41, 45

disease(s) 6-20, 22-23, 35, 39; causes of: damp air, 8; evil spirits, 19; germ theory of, 9, 10, 11

doctor(s) 5-8, 10-11, 17, 20-21, 24, 26-29, 34-35, 36, 41-45, 47

drug(s) 19-21, 28-29: opium, 26; painkilling, 5, 30. *See also* anaesthetic(s); miracle drugs

Einhorn, Alfred 30, 46

electronics 41-42: electronic parts, 42

ether anaesthesia 27, 28, 29, 46

Everest, Mount 43, 47

Faraday, Michael 27, 46

Fleming, Alexander 19, 46

flesh-eating disease 22

foreign objects 35

fungus 19

genes 17, 45

genetic form 21

genetically engineered plants 17

germ(s) 5- 9, 10, 11, 12, 14, 19-22

hand washing 6-8, 10, 11

health-care professionals 11

heart 36, 45

Herodotus 39

hospitals 8, 23, 24

Hounsfield, Godfrey 37, 47

human waste 7, 9
hygiene 9

illness 7, 19, 21
immunity 12-14
infection 6, 7, 18-22, 23:
  of ear, 18; infected wounds,
  20-21, 44
influenza (the flu), 17
Inglis, Mark 43, 47
injection 14-15, 17, 31
injury 19, 21, 41, 43-44
invention(s) 5-10, 15, 23-24, 40-41,

Jenner, Edward 13-15, 46

knives 5, 25
Koch, Robert 10, 11, 46

laboratory 17, 19, 21, 46
laughing gas. *See* nitrous oxide
Leeuwenhoek, Anton van 8, 46
limbs, artificial 38-43, 45, 47; control
  of, 39, 41-43; oldest ever found, 39;
  phantom, 41; Utah Arm, 42, 47
limbs, prosthetic (artificial). *See* limbs,
  artificial
Lister, Joseph 10, 46
Long, Crawford 27, 28

maternity ward 8
measles 17, 47
mechanical parts 42

medical: discoveries 7; inventions, 5;
  staff, 29; students, 11, 28
medicine(s) 18-19, 24, 26, 30
micro-organisms 7. *See also* bacteria;
  germs; viruses
milkmaid(s) 12, 13
miracle drugs 5, 18-19
Morton, William 28-29, 46
mould 5, 19-20, 21. *See also*
  antibiotic(s); Penicillium notatum
mumps 17
myoelectricity 41-42, 47

nitrous oxide 27-29, 46
novocaine 30, 31, 46

operating: rooms 10-11; table,
  25
operation(s) 5, 25-26, 28
organs 36, 45

Pare, Ambroise 40
Parmelee, Dubois 41, 46
Pasteur, Louis 9, 10, 11, 15, 46
patient(s) 11, 26-28
peg (wooden) legs 38-40
  See also limbs, artificial
Penicillium notatum (penicillin) 19-
  21, 27, 46
PET scan. *See* positron emission
  tomography
Phipps, James 13-14, 46
pneumonia 20, 23

polio 16, 46. *See also* Salk, Jonas

positron emission tomography (PET scanning) 36

prevention 7, 15, 16-17

prosthetics 39, 42-43. *See also* limbs, artificial

puerperal fever 8. *See also* hand washing; infection

pus 6, 12-14. *See also* infection

radiation 33

Roentgen, Wilhelm 33-34, 35, 46

Roosevelt, Franklin D 16

Sabin, Albert 16, 46

Salk, Jonas 16, 46: and polio vaccine, 16-17. *See also* vaccination(s) and vaccine(s)

scarlet fever 20

Semmelweis, Ignaz 8-9, 46

side effects 14, 21, 28

smallpox 12-15, 17, 46

sodium pentothal 28-29, 31, 46

staphylococcus bacteria (staph) 7, 19, 20, 22

sterilize 11

stomach 24, 36: ulcers, 24, 47. *See also* bacteria

streptomycin 21, 46. *See also* antibiotic(s)

super bugs 21, 22

surgeon(s) 10, 26-29, 35, 40

surgery 10-11, 24, 26-29, 35

Tabern, Donalee 28, 46

teeth and tooth decay 31, 35

tuberculosis (TB) 15, 21, 35, 46

US Centers for Disease Control and Prevention (CDC) 8

vaccination(s) and vaccine(s) 12-14, 15, 16-17, 46

virus(es) 7, 12, 16, 17, 20

Volwiler, Ernest 28, 46

Waksman, Selman 21, 46

Warren, John Collins 25

wars 39, 41: US Civil War, 41; World War I, 41; World War II, 20, 21

Wells, Horace 28, 46

X-rays 32-37, 46: dangers of, 37; x-ray vision 35

COVER AND CHAPTER OPENER PHOTO CAPTIONS

cover Top: A man receives surgery on his arm without anaesthesia in the 1600s. Bottom: Surgeons operate on a fully anaesthetized patient during the 2000s.

pp 4–5 A surgeon operates on a patient during the late 1400s.

p 6 An operation in progress during the 1800s. The patient is held down because the operation takes place without anaesthesia.

p 12 Nurses tend to smallpox sufferers in Britain during the early 1800s.

p 18 Penicillin *(centre)* stops the growth of pneumonia virus *(clear area around the penicillin)* in a petri dish.

p 25 A patient withstands the agonizing pain of cauterization (burning a wound shut) without anaesthesia in the 1600s.

p 32 A boy lies on an X-ray table in 1915. X-ray machines allow doctors to look inside the body without cutting.

p 38 This 1750 illustration shows assistants restraining a man while a doctor saws off the man's diseased arm.

pp 44–45 Medical nanobots make their way through the human blood stream to fight disease in this artist's illustration of the theoretical machines.

ABOUT THE AUTHORS
Michael Woods is a science and medical journalist who has won many national writing awards. He works in the National Bureau of the *Pittsburgh Post-Gazette* and *Toledo Blade* newspapers. Mary B. Woods has worked as a librarian in the Fairfax County Public School System in Virginia and at the Benjamin Franklin International School in Barcelona, Spain. The Woodses' previous books include the eight-volume Ancient Technology series. The Woodses have four children and two grandchildren.

PHOTO ACKNOWLEDGEMENTS
The images in this book are used with the permission of: © Montgomery Ward & Co., p 1, all borders; © Hulton Archive/Getty Images, pp 4–5, 6, 12, 25; © Dr Dennis Kunkel/Visuals Unlimited, p 7; Library of Congress, pp 9, 14 (LC-USZC4-3147), 15 (LC-USZC2-5173), 23 (LC-USZC2-5391), 29 (LC-USZ62-67905), 30 (LC-USZ62-68282); Courtesy The National Library of Medicine, pp 10, 16, 20, 26, 27, 34, 38; © Time Life Pictures/Getty Images, p 11; © Bettmann/CORBIS, p 13; © Fred Marsik/Visuals Unlimited, p 18; © Dr Ken Greer/Visuals Unlimited, p 22; © Eliot J. Schechter/Getty Images, p 24; © Royalty-Free/CORBIS, p 31; © Lewis W. Hine/George Eastman House/Getty Images, p 32; Mayo Clinic Library, p 33; © Simon Fraser/Freeman Hospital, Newcastle Upon Tyne/Science Photo Library/Photo Researchers, p 36; © Egyptian Antiquity Department/Handout/Reuters/CORBIS, p 37; © MPI/Getty Images, p 40; Courtesy Motion Control, Inc., p 42; © Digital Art/CORBIS pp 44–45.

Front cover: top, Courtesy Library New York Academy of Medicine; bottom, © Tom Stewart/CORBIS. Montgomery Ward & Co., back cover, p 1, all borders